Contents

British Library Cataloguing in Publication Data

Play songs
    1. Children's action songs in English. Words — Anthologies
I. Finnigan, Helen   II. Langton, Roger
784.6′2405
ISBN 0-7214-1167-3

First edition

Published by Ladybird Books Ltd Loughborough Leicestershire UK
Ladybird Books Inc Auburn Maine 04210 USA

Printed in England

Ladybird Action Rhymes

Play songs

compiled by Helen Finnigan
illustrated by Roger Langton

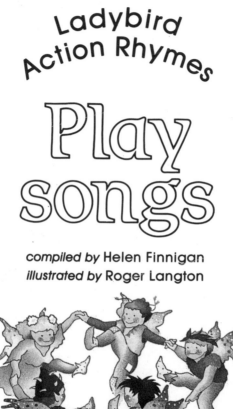

Ladybird Books

Oh, the grand old Duke of York,
He had ten thousand men,
He marched them up to the top of the hill,
And he marched them down again.

4

Chorus
And when they were up they were up,
And when they were down they were down,
And when they were only halfway up,
They were neither up nor down.

Children stand in a line across the room.
Verse:
lines 1 and 2, march on the spot;
line 3, advance marching;
line 4, march backward.
Chorus:
line 1, march forward;
line 2, march backward;
lines 3 and 4, march forward with tiny steps.

Chorus (to follow each verse)
Here we go Looby Loo,
Here we go Looby Light,
Here we go Looby Loo,
All on a Saturday night.

You put your right arm in,
You put your right arm out,
You shake it a little, a little,
And turn yourself about.

6

You put your left arm in,
You put your left arm out,
You shake it a little, a little,
And turn yourself about.

You put your right leg in,
You put your right leg out,
You shake it a little, a little,
And turn yourself about.

You put your left leg in, *etc*.

You put your whole self in, *etc*.

I sent a letter to my love
And on the way I dropped it;
One of you has picked it up
And put it in your pocket.
A-dree, a-dree, I dropped it.

*All children except one sit down in a ring. The chosen
one runs round the outside while the song is sung and
drops a handkerchief behind one of the seated
children on the word 'dropped it'.*

*The seated child picks up the handkerchief, and
chases the first child round the outside of the ring. If
the first child reaches the vacant space in the ring
without being caught, he or she sits down there, the
game continues, and the song is sung again.*

Sally go round the stars,
Sally go round the moon,
Sally go round the chimney pots
     on a Sunday afternoon. Oop.

...on a *Monday* afternoon, *etc*.

Children all join hands in a ring and dance round in a clockwise direction. At 'Oop', the right leg is kicked up as high as possible. For the next verse, kick left leg and dance in the opposite direction.

Skip, skip, skip to my Lou,
Skip, skip, skip to my Lou,
Skip, skip, skip to my Lou,
Skip to my Lou, my darling.

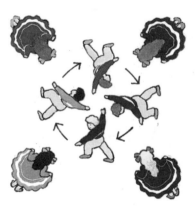

Partner's gone, what will I do?
Partner's gone, what will I do?
Partner's gone, what will I do?
Skip to my Lou, my darling.

Fly in the sugar bowl, shoo shoo shoo,
Fly in the sugar bowl, shoo shoo shoo,
Fly in the sugar bowl, shoo shoo shoo,
Skip to my Lou, my darling.

Little red wagon painted blue, *etc.*

Cow in the meadow, moo moo moo, *etc.*

*Two circles are formed, one inside the other, boys on
the inside, girls on the outside. Each faces his or her
partner, holding hands.*
Chorus: All skip round.
Verse 1: Girls stand still while boys skip round.
*Chorus: Each boy takes a new partner and game
        continues as before.*

In and out the dusky bluebells
In and out the dusky bluebells
In and out the dusky bluebells
You shall be my partner.

Tippety tappety on my shoulder
Tippety tappety on my shoulder
Tippety tappety on my shoulder
You shall be my partner.

Verse 1:
Children make a ring with joined hands in form of arches. One child skips in and out of the arches.

Verse 2:
The child stops behind one of his or her choice. The ring then closes and chosen child skips off holding onto back of first child. Verses 1 and 2 (actions) are repeated and third child chosen. Game is repeated until all the children are forming a chain, when they all skip round singing for as long as they like.

The farmer's in his den,
The farmer's in his den,
E——I——E——I,
The farmer's in his den.

The farmer wants a wife,
The farmer wants a wife,
E——I——E——I,
The farmer wants a wife.

Verse 1: Children form a ring. A child, as farmer, skips around the middle of the ring, while others skip and sing.
Verse 2: Farmer chooses a wife and takes her into the middle.
Verse 3: Wife chooses a child, etc.

The wife wants a child,
The wife wants a child,
E——I——E——I,
The wife wants a child.

The child wants a nurse, *etc.*

The nurse wants a dog, *etc.*

The dog wants a bone, *etc.*

We all pat the bone, *etc.*

Verse 4: Child chooses a nurse, etc.
Verse 5: Nurse chooses a dog, etc.
Verse 6: Dog chooses a bone, etc.
Verse 7: Everyone gently pats the bone, who becomes the farmer when the game starts again.

The big ship sails down the Ally Ally O,
The Ally Ally O, the Ally Ally O,
The big ship sails down the Ally Ally O,
On the last day of September.

The big ship sails too slow, too slow,
Too slow, too slow, too slow, too slow,
The big ship sails too slow, too slow,
On the last day of September.

The Captain said, 'It will never, never do,
Never never do, never never do,'
The Captain said, 'It will never, never do,'
On the last day of September.

The big ship sank to the bottom of the sea,
The bottom of the sea, the bottom of the sea,
The big ship sank to the bottom of the sea,
On the last day of September.

We all dip our heads in the deep blue sea,
The deep blue sea, the deep blue sea,
We all dip our heads in the deep blue sea,
On the last day of September.

All children hold hands in a long line. One child at the end puts his arm up against a wall to make an arch.

The child at the other end leads the rest of the line under the arch so that the child making the arch twists round until his or her arms are crossed.

This is repeated while the first verse only is sung again and again until all children have crossed arms.

Verse 2: First and last child form ring by joining their crossed hands. Verse is sung at slow speed.

Verse 3: Shake heads gravely.

Verse 4: Slowly squat and rise again.

Verse 5: Bend heads down as low as possible.

Little sister dance with me,
Dance with me so merrily,
One foot in, one foot out,
Once and twice and turn about.

Well done sister, try once more,
Turn around me as before,
One foot in, one foot out,
Once and twice and turn about.

For each verse:
Each child takes a partner and they proceed clockwise round the room.

Lines 1-2:
Walk round the room with inside hands joined, swinging in time to the music and outside hands on hips.

Join us in our dancing song,
We will dance the whole day long,
One foot in, one foot out,
Once and twice and turn about.

Line 3:
Stop with feet together, tap first with the left foot and then with the right.

Line 4:
Join both hands with partner into a circle, walk round until back in your place. Drop outside hands, ready to begin again.

Heads, shoulders, knees and toes,
Knees and toes,
Heads, shoulders, knees and toes,
Knees and toes,
And eyes and ears and mouth and nose,
Heads, shoulders, knees and toes,
Knees and toes.

Actions:

First time:
Touch each part of the body as it is mentioned.

Second time:
Keep action going but omit the word 'heads'.

Third time:
Keep pointing to each part as mentioned but omit saying 'heads' or 'shoulders'.

Fourth time:
Omit saying 'heads', 'shoulders' and 'knees', and so on until there are no words left – only actions.

Oh dear, what can the matter be?
Oh dear, what can the matter be?
Oh dear, what can the matter be?
Johnny's so long at the fair.

He promised to buy me
        a bunch of blue ribbons –
He promised to buy me
        a bunch of blue ribbons –
He promised to buy me
        a bunch of blue ribbons –
To tie up my bonnie brown hair.

Skipping songs

On a mountain stands a lady,
Who she is I do not know,
All she wants is gold and silver,
All she wants is a nice young man.

Mrs Brown went to town
Riding on a pony.
When she came back
She lost her hat
And called on Miss Maloney.

Skipping songs

Up the ladder and down the wall,
Penny an hour will serve us all.
You buy butter and I'll buy flour,
And we'll have a pudding in half an hour.
With...salt...mustard...vinegar...pepper, *etc*.

Half a pound of tuppenny rice,
Half a pound of treacle.
That's the way the money goes –
Pop goes the Weasel!

Oranges and lemons,
Say the bells of St Clement's;
You owe me five farthings,
Say the bells of St Martin's;
When will you pay me?
Say the bells at Old Bailey;
When I grow rich,
Say the bells at Shoreditch;
When will that be?
Say the bells at Stepney;
I'm sure I don't know,
Says the Great Bell at Bow.

Here comes a candle to light you to bed;
Here comes a chopper to chop off
your head.

*The rope is held by two players, one of whom is
'Oranges' and the other 'Lemons'. The others skip in
turn, and when one makes a mistake, he or she
whispers 'Oranges' or 'Lemons' and joins in behind the
chosen leader. When all are out, there is a tug of war.*

Chorus (to follow each verse)
Here we go round the mulberry bush,
The mulberry bush, the mulberry bush,
Here we go round the mulberry bush
On a cold and frosty morning.

This is the way we wash our hands,
Wash our hands, wash our hands,
This is the way we wash our hands
On a cold and frosty morning.

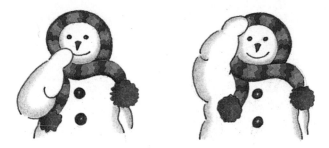

This is the way we wash our face,
Wash our face, wash our face,
This is the way we wash our face
On a cold and frosty morning.

This is the way we comb our hair,
Comb our hair, comb our hair,
This is the way we comb our hair
On a cold and frosty morning.

This is the way we tie our shoes, *etc*.

This is the way we go to school, *etc*.

Chorus: All children skip round in a ring, holding hands.
Verse: They stand still and perform the action.